Cozy Country Cabins

Published by Upgraded Books

Copyright © 2023 Upgraded Books

All rights reserved. No part of this book may be reproduced or used in any manner without the prior written permission of the copyright owner of this book.

Thank you so much for choosing my coloring book! Your support means the world to me.

I am the founder of Upgraded Books -- a small business dedicated to bringing calm and joy to the world through books. :)

Every purchase and every colorful page really brightens my day and I would love to share my other labors of love with you!

Whether you're in need of relaxation, seeking inspiration, or simply craving a good laugh, I have a coloring book that matches your mood.

Love,
Simone

This Belongs To

_____

www.ingramcontent.com/pod-product-compliance
Lightning Source LLC
Chambersburg PA
CBHW081622100526
44590CB00021B/3556